Build Your Modern Doll House with Bowed Window

Plan Book: 2 Floors, 6 Room Modern Doll House

By Dollhouse Devotions

All rights reserved.

No part of this publication may be reproduced in any form or by any means, including scanning, photocopying, or otherwise without prior written permission of the copyright holder.

Disclaimer and Terms of Use: The Author and Publisher has strived to be as accurate and complete as possible in the creation of this book, notwithstanding the fact that he does not warrant or represent at any time that the contents within are accurate due to the rapidly changing nature of the Internet. While all attempts have been made to verify information provided in this publication, the Author and Publisher assumes no responsibility for errors, omissions, or contrary interpretation of the subject matter herein.

As with any craft book, care needs to be taken when working with anything sharp, chemical based or anything else craft related. The Author and Publisher are not responsible for any injury relating to the use of craft supplies.

You are given a non-transferable, "personal use" license to this product. You cannot distribute it or share it with other individuals.

Also, there are no resale rights or private label rights granted when purchasing this document. In other words, it's for your own personal use only.

The original illustrations and plans for this book came from works by Robert Nealy. Additional illustrations and updated instructions have been provided by Dollhouse Devotions.

Build Your Own Modern Doll House with Bowed Window

Plan Book: 2 Floors, 6 Room Modern Doll House

By Dollhouse Devotions

Table of Contents

Introduction 7
General Instructions 10

    Patterns 10
    Foam Core 11
    Wood 11
    Nails 12
    Illustration Board 13
    Turnings 14
    Trim 16

House with Bowed Window 17

    Important Info 18
    The Layout 20
    The Ground Floor 23
    First Floor 25
    Front 27
    Back 29
    Ends 32
    Partitions 34
    Partitions Ground Floor 34
    Partitions First Floor 38
    Windows 39
    Bowed Window 43
    Railings 52
    Roof 54
    Chimney 56
    Front Door 58
    Assembly 59

Finishing Touches 60

    Floors 60
    Wall Pictures 62
    Brick 63
    Shingles 64
    Doors 64
    Stained Glass 65
    Wallpaper 65

Introduction

From simple one-room cottages, to log cabins, to Colleen Moore's Fairy Tale Castle, there's just something about a dollhouse that appeals to the child in us all.

In days gone by, the dollhouse was a true work of art, something you would be proud to display to friends and family. They were the realms of adults, not children.

These days, there are more 'kit' houses available than ever before. However, the modern miniaturist isn't looking for a kit house. The dollhouse collector and artist wants something more challenging, more inspirational.

They want something more like the dollhouses of days gone by. They want a dollhouse that's a work of art.

This book series will introduce you to some of the most popular and the most unusual dollhouses of days gone by.

These books have been specially designed to look like a plan book from yesteryear. From their creamy papers to their charming hand drawn illustrations, to their faux woven cover, everything is designed to give you an experience like few other books can.

Important info will be at the beginning of each project. It will give you a list of materials, the difficulty level, the size of the house according to the measurements and how easy it can be replicated in foam core.

At the end of each book there are some easy decorating ideas such as hardwood floors and carpets and shingles.

Every lover of dollhouses wants a dollhouse as beautiful and unique as the treasures it contains and this book will provide hours of fun as you create the perfect dollhouse for all your treasures.

****

As a crafter and dollhouse lover myself, I know what a hassle it is to try to copy patterns out of books.

That's why I've included a link that enables you to download all the patterns in this book in reduced size PDF form.

You can use your computer or copier to adjust them to whatever size you need.

Simply scan the QR code below or go to this website to get your PDF patterns:

http://www.thisofferisgreat.com/dhmodern

General Instructions

Patterns

This book contains patterns and illustrations for all the dollhouses.

The patterns in this series come in a variety sizes. While many are for 1:12 houses, others are not.

Fortunately, you can actually make these houses any size you want by making minor adjustments and enlarging the pattern to the size you need.

While measurements don't need to be quite as exact as the ones given here, precise measurements do give a wonderful 'starting point' for your ultimate creation.

Go here to download the patterns for this book.

http://www.thisofferisgreat.com/dhmodern

Foam Core

Though traditional dollhouses are made of wood, I have always preferred foam core due to its ease of use. The instructions for each house are for wood. However, they can also be made out of foam core with relative ease. For each house, I mention the level of difficulty involved with following the instructions to turn it into a foam core house rather than a wooden one.

Wood

It all starts with the wood. What kind of wood you choose is ultimately decided by what kind of dollhouse you want. A dollhouse that will be completely covered in wallpaper and brick can use very rough wood, such as plywood. However, a dollhouse that's going to be finely finished and painted should use a wood of higher quality.

The highest quality wood for dollhouses is basswood. Even though it's among the most expensive, the finished result is truly an heirloom quality house.

If price is a concern, you can choose less-expensive wood, like pine. Pine can still give you a finely finished heirloom quality dollhouse for a fraction of the cost of basswood. Additionally, being a soft wood, it's still very easy to work with.

The most important thing to remember when working with pine or other woods is to make sure it's free from knots and other out of scale defects that could ruin the overall look of your perfect house.

Nails

Because this is not a real house, we can use smaller nails that leave easy to fill holes.

While screws will give you the sturdiest house, finishing nails will give you an overall smooth appearance and can be punched in with an awl.

Once punched in, finishing nails are easily covered up with a little bit of wood putty, sandpaper and paint.

Illustration Board

Illustration board is available at many fine art stores and is wonderful for a variety of purposes. Illustration board is actually a type of compressed cardboard. It is sturdy and easy to cut with a craft knife.

Illustration board is easy to curve around things. To curve illustration board, use a craft knife to lightly score the illustration board as shown by the dotted lines below.

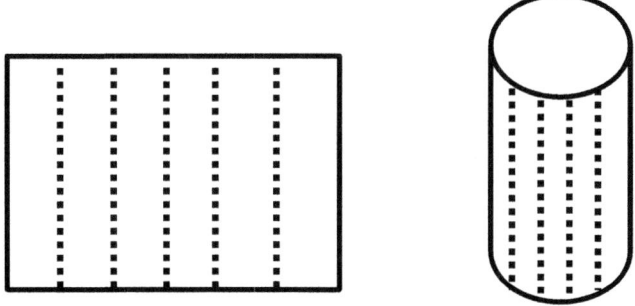

Once you've scored the illustration board, curve the illustration board away from the lines instead of toward.

This method can be used for creating columns, arches, tubes and bowed windows.

Cardstock can then be wrapped around the piece and finished as desired.

Turnings

Throughout this book, you'll notice references to 'turnings'. Turnings are fancy, 3 dimensional, freestanding, carved woodwork.

Example of turnings

Turnings can be used in a variety of places in your dollhouse, including:

- Stair railings
- Poster Beds
- Architectural columns
- Furniture legs
- More...

In this book, we use them primarily for creating railings for stairs.

Real wood turnings can be bought relatively cheaply at just about any dollhouse supply store or catalogue.

You can find a section of online resources in the back of the books where you can buy turnings.

However, for the truly creative, you can use beads to simulate wood turnings.

These beads can be either wood or plastic. Carved beads, such as ethnic beads make a particularly good looking carved 'turning'.

Simply stack beads on top of each other until you get the size and shape that you want. Glue them in place. Then paint the beads to resemble wood.

Just like with wood turnings, these bead 'turnings' can give you a wonderful effect and can be used for furniture feet, elaborate carvings, columns and posters on a four poster

Turning made from beads

15

bed.

Trim

Trim can go either on the inside or outside of the dollhouse. It can be the molding next to the floorboards, the ceiling or the outside of the house.

It can also go around the windows, doors and porches.

Though you can buy regular wood trim from your favorite dollhouse retailer, there are other ways to simulate trim.

Heavily textured lace or embossed papers work well as trim. In addition, lace has the added benefit of being able to bend around curves and corners without needing to be mitered.

Deeply Etched Lace

Heavily textured lace, like the lace in the picture, works best for this.

Modern Doll House with Bowed Window

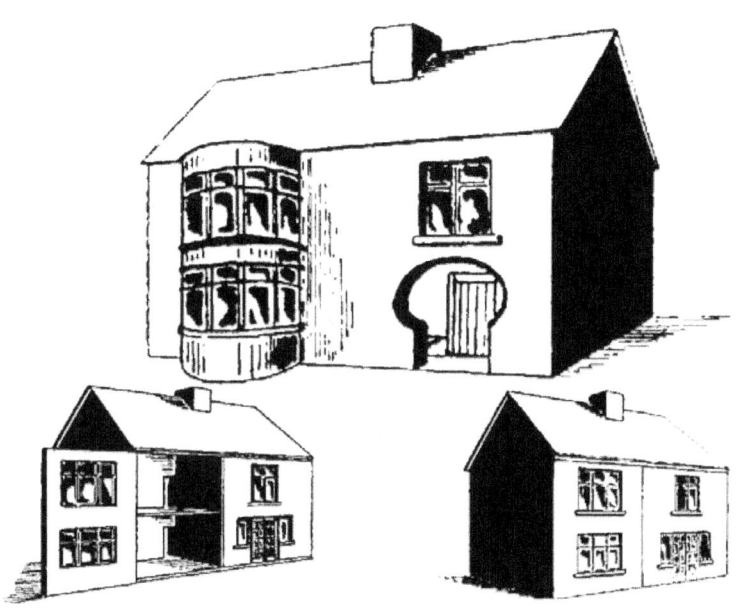

Important Info:

Size of house:
- 2.5 feet long, 1 foot wide and 2.5 feet high

Level of difficulty:
- Intermediate to advanced

Can be reproduced in foam core:
- Easily

Materials:
- Sheets of wood (and tools for wood)
- Glue
- Strip wood
- Plastic sheet glass
- Toothpicks/dowels
- Illustration board (board)
- Cardstock (Card)
- T-square (or carpenters ruler)
- Pencil

Though basically a colonial style house, this dollhouse is much more challenging.

Because of its bowed front and bulbous door opening, this house is more architecturally interesting than a simple colonial house.

However, this home is easier than it looks. Unlike some of the other houses in this series, this house is assembled at the end rather than as you go.

The Layout

Because of the bulbous entryway, this house actually has a tiny courtyard before arriving at the actual interior of the dollhouse.

That's why there is a separate plan for the ground floor (figure 1) and the first floor (figure 2).

The plan for the ground floor has a tiny courtyard, while the plan for the first floor has a slight overhang.

The layout is for laying out the partitions and other features. The actual 'base' of the house is the true pattern.

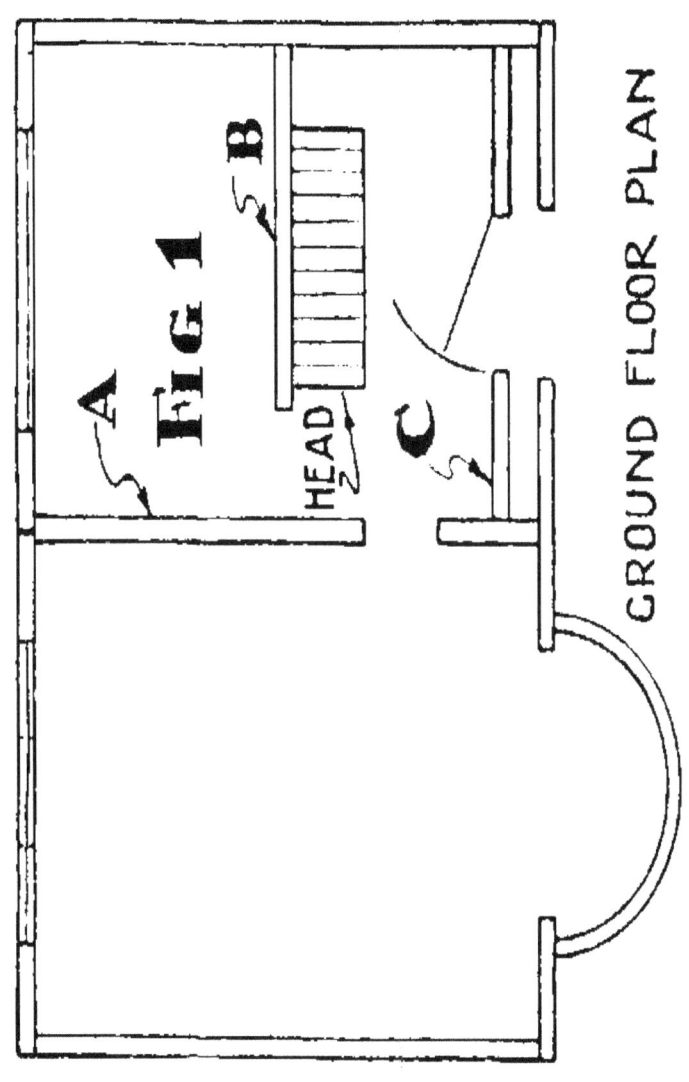

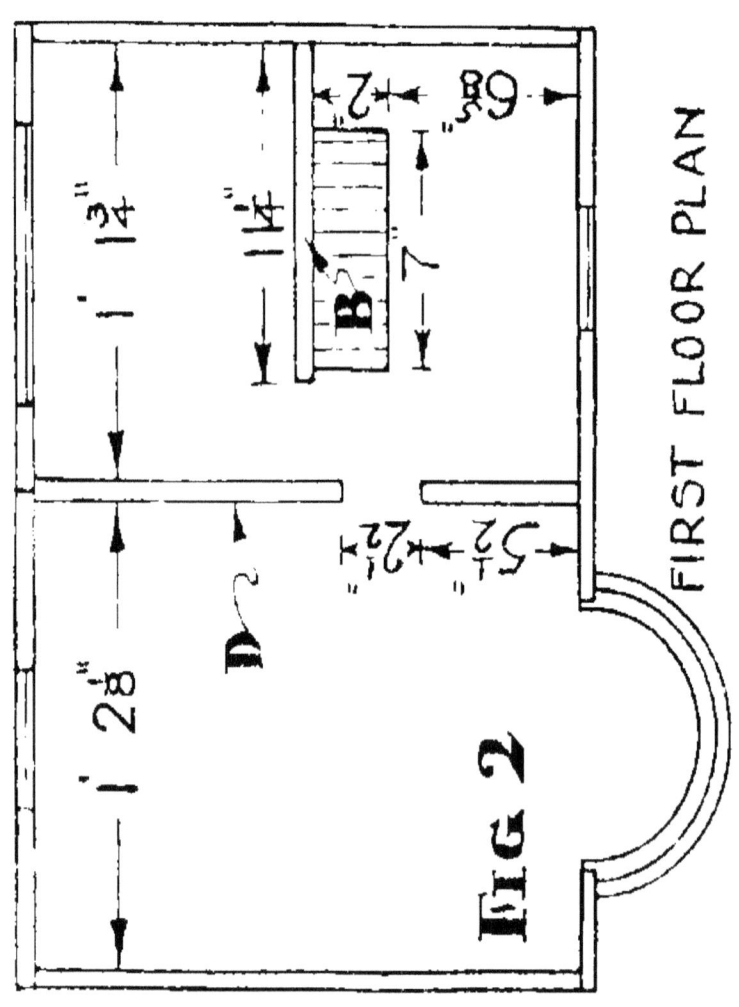

The Ground Floor

The ground floor is 2.5' x 2'

This design has no false basement so the dollhouse will be sitting directly on this bottom board.

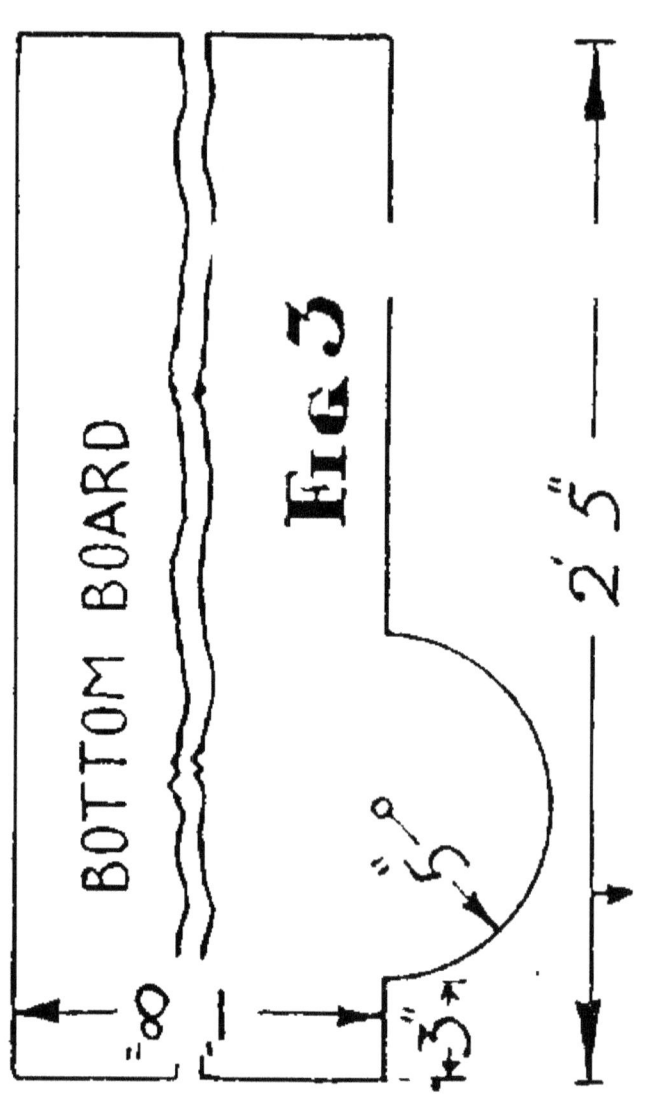

First Floor

The pattern for the first floor is figure 4. It's almost identical to the base pattern, except for the hole.

This hole is where the stairs will go. There are many ways to make this hole. The simplest is by building the floor in two pieces with the appropriate measurements as shown in figure 4.

Cut the hole before attaching the two pieces together to avoid uneven edges.

If you still have uneven edges, take a couple of small pieces of strip wood and finish off the hole after the flooring is installed. This will give your hole a finished look and add to your house's charm.

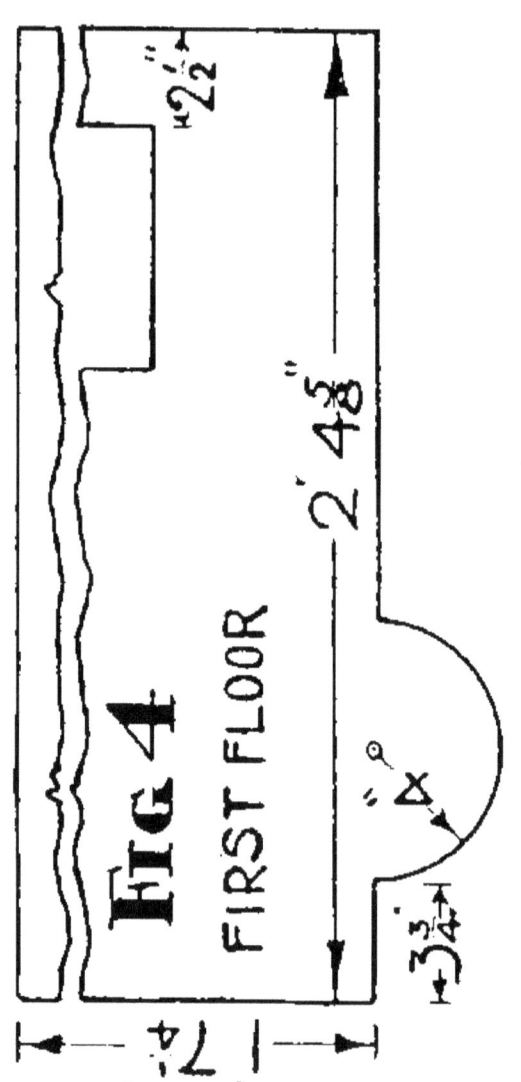

Fig. 4
FIRST FLOOR

Front

The front of the house 2'5" x 1'6"

Mark and cut the windows the same way you did for the stairs on the first floor.

Don't worry if your windows have uneven edges. The window frames will hide them later.

The front of this house has a doorway with a bulbous opening.

Since this was done purely for architectural aesthetics, you can easily change this to rectangular or even pointed if you choose to.

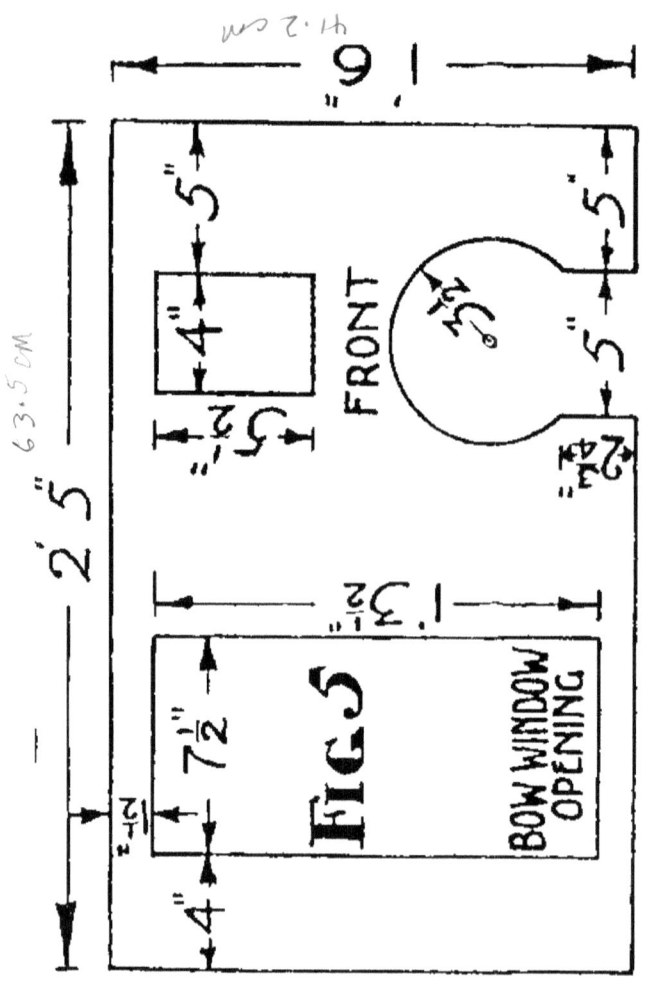

Back

Unlike many kit dollhouses, this dollhouse has a hinged back.

This is common of traditional European dollhouses. Though they were finished on all sides, they were not elaborately finished.

American dollhouses have open backs to allow for elaborate porches and landscaping on the front.

Adding this back is entirely optional. If you don't want to add it, you can leave the back open.

If you decide to leave the back open, you can skip this next step.

If you decide you want to make a traditional European dollhouse with a hinged back, this is how you do it.

The back is made up of the strip of wood 2'5" x 1.5'. This forms the portion of the wall that is under the roof.

There are also two larger pieces.

The first is 1' x 2 11/16" x 1' x 4'5"

The second is 1' 2 5/16" x 1' 4 1/2."

These parts will swing open.

Cut three window openings and the door opening shown in figure 6 before installing.

To install the back use small hinges from any hardware store.

Now your hinged back is complete.

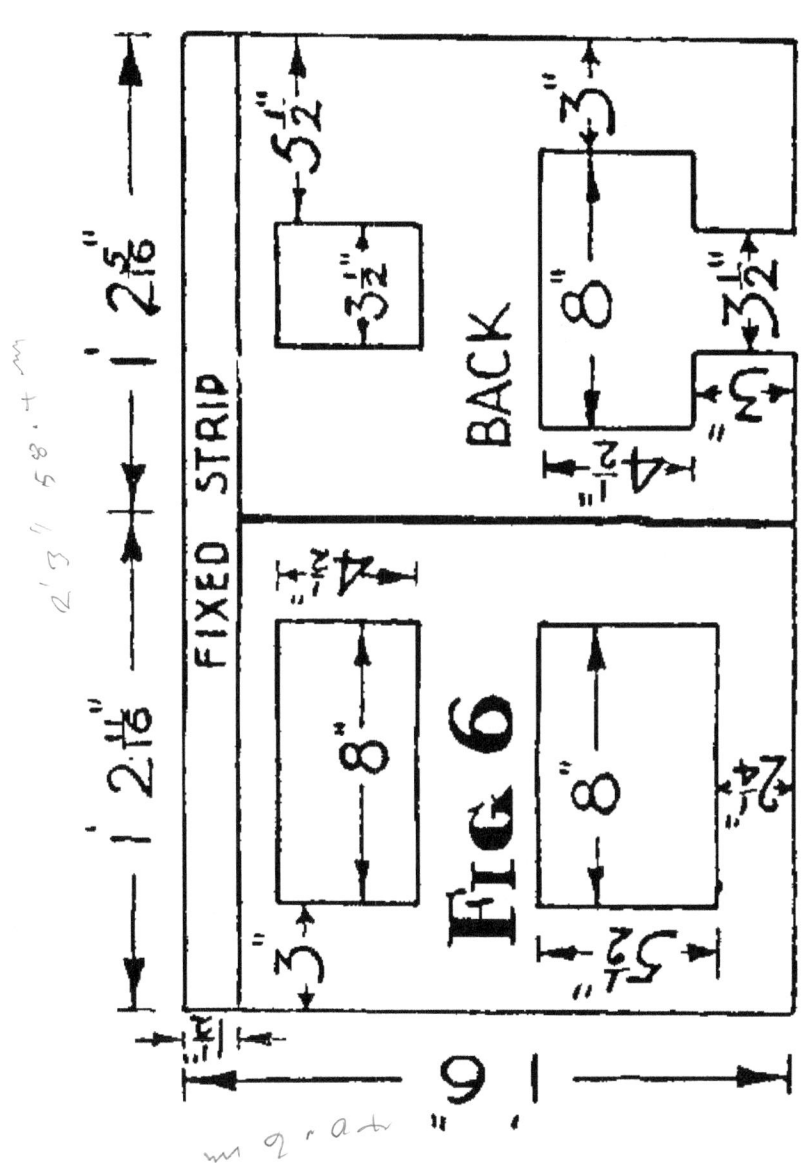

Ends

There are no windows on the ends of the house, so the ends are very easy to make.

Cut two pieces for the ends from the thickest wood you have. These ends will have grooves carved into them later, so the thicker, the better.

Each end should be 2' 4" x 1' 8."

Because this house is asymmetrical, one side should be square and the other triangular.

A groove carved into the ends gives the floors the added support they need.

These grooves can be made with a chisel.

The grooves should be about 3/8" wide and 3/16" deep as shown on figure 7.

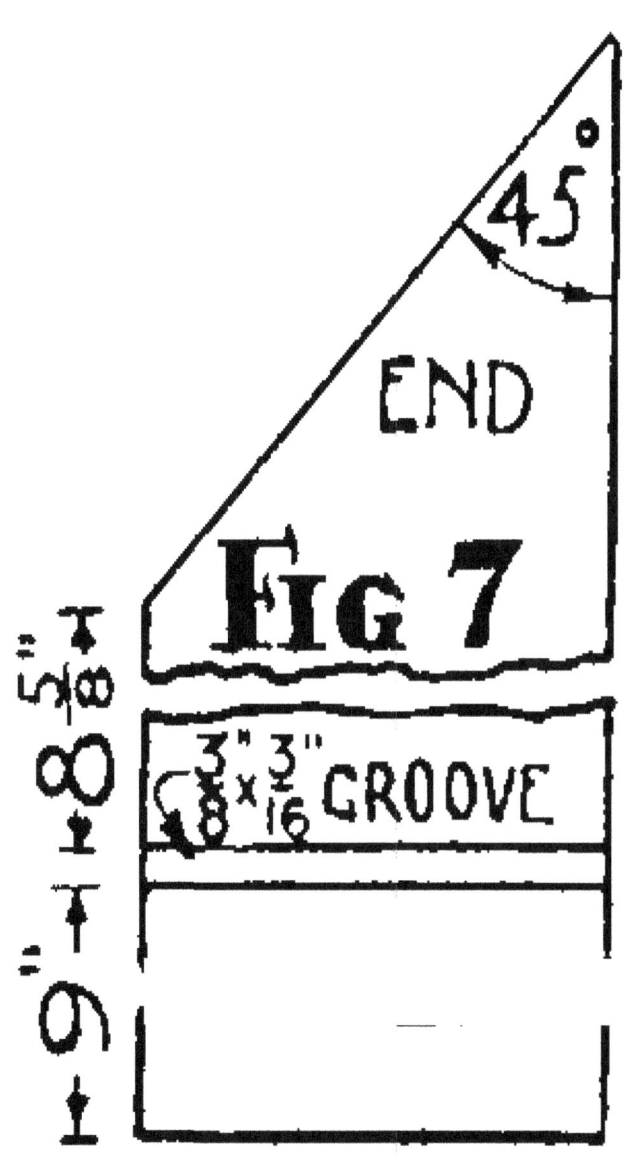

Partitions

The partitions in this house can be divided anyway you like. The plan shows that the ground floor has three partitions while the first floor has only two.

The number of partitions can be changed according to your preference.

Partitions Ground Floor

There are three partitions for the ground floor, A, B and C.

Partition A is 1' 7 ¼" x 9."

The opening is 6" x 2 1/2."

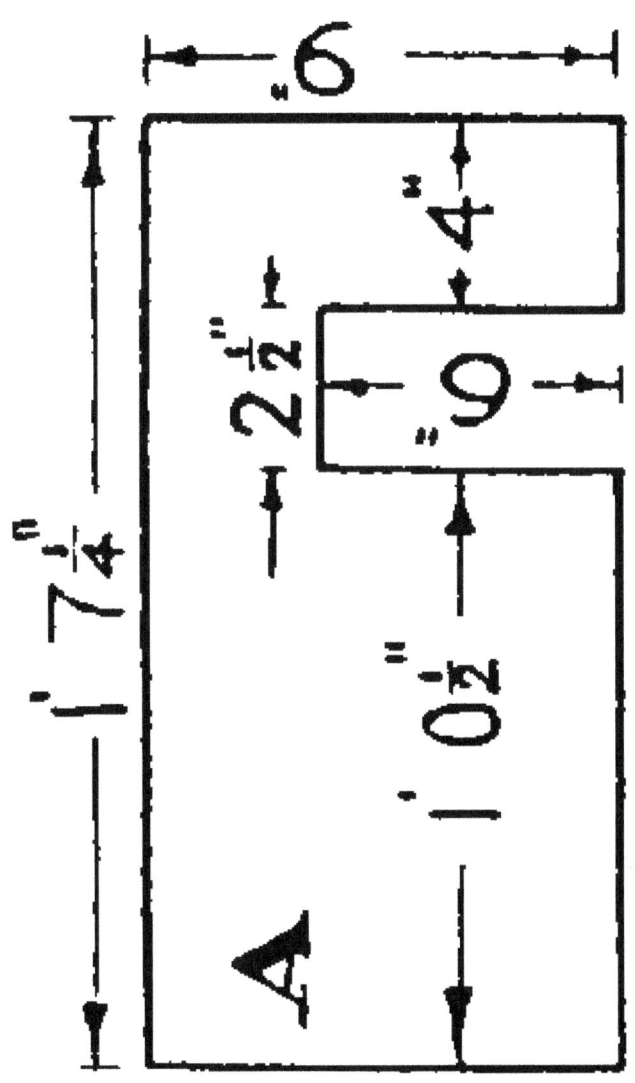

Partition B is 1' 1 3/4" x 9."

There is a piece cut out of one corner that measures 6" x 2 ½."

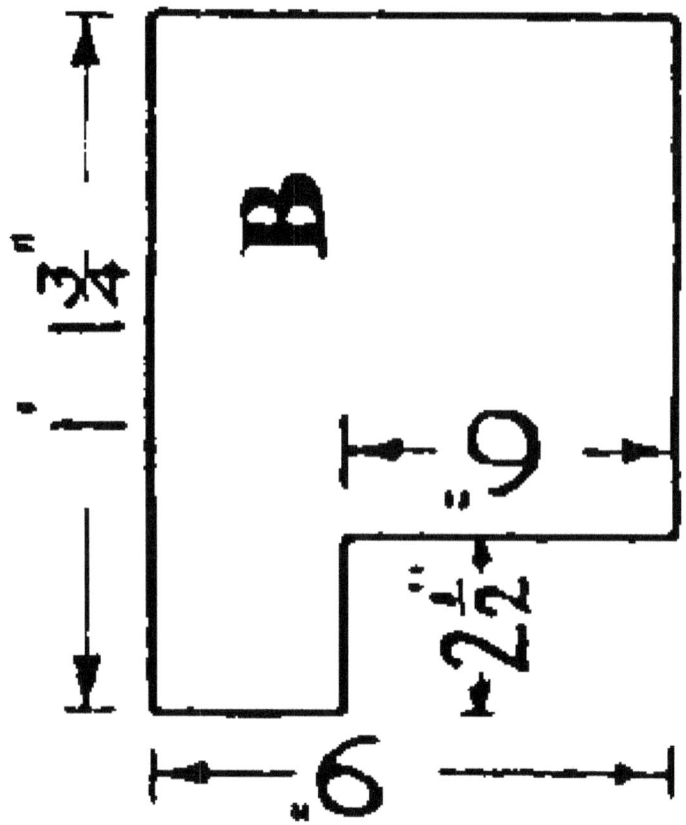

Partition C is 1' 1 ¾" x 9."

The main difference between B and C is that this opening is 6" x 4"

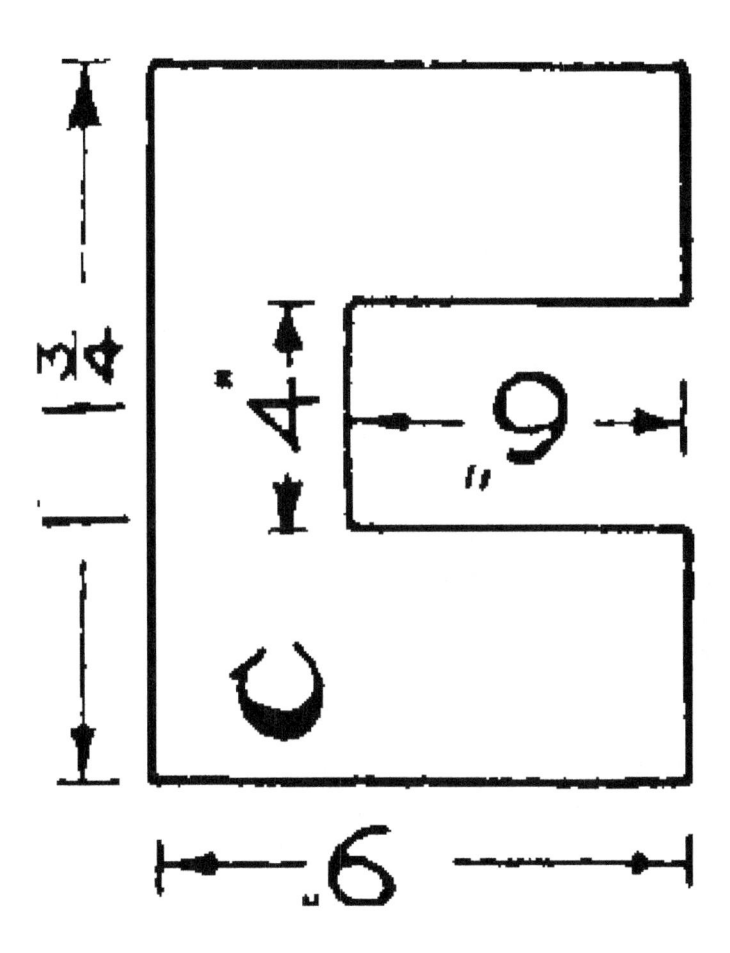

Partitions First Floor

There are two first floor partitions; B again and a new one, D. As in both pictures, cut the openings as shown.

Partition B is 1' x 1 3/4" x 9." There is a piece cut out of one corner. It measures 6" x 2 ½."

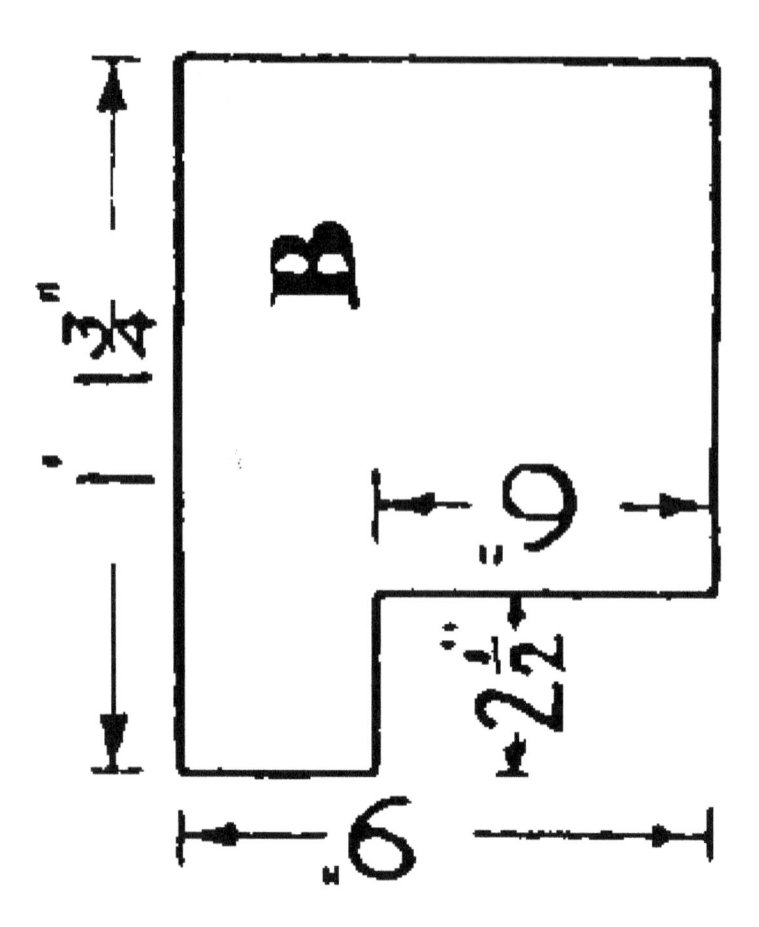

Partition D is 1' 7 ¼" x 9." The opening is 6" x 2 ½".

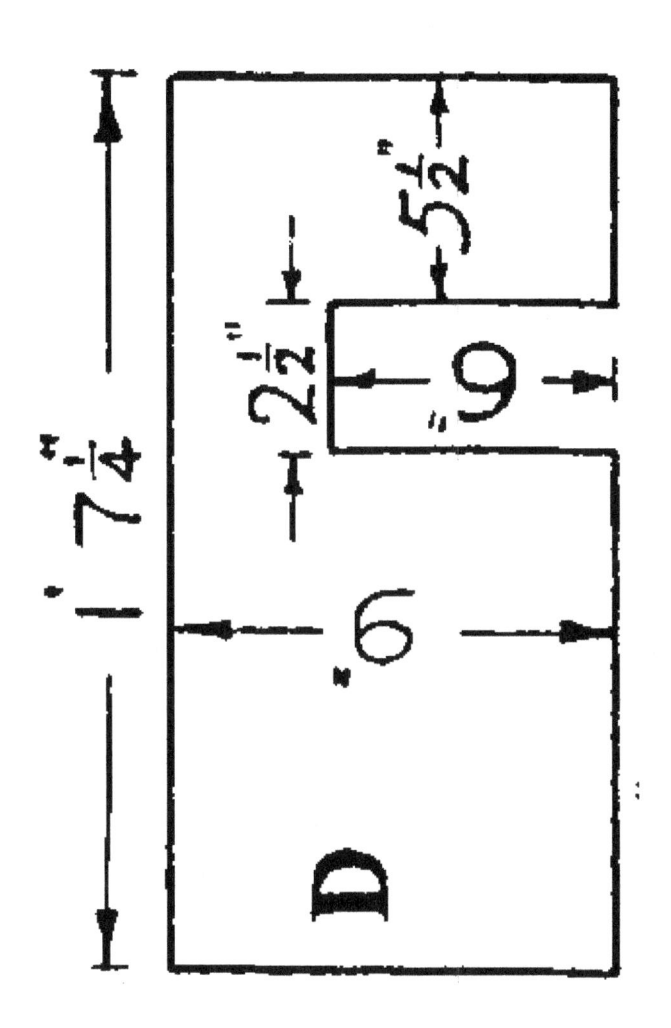

Windows

Naturally, you can buy pre-made windows but here I'm going to show you how to make your own, including the glass.

Simply use strip wood or illustration board to make window casements as shown in the pattern below.

Window 'glass' for dollhouses can be easily purchased. It's sold as sheets of thin plastic.

This plastic sheet (sometime known as 'plastic sheet glass) is easily cut with a craft knife or scissors.

Cut the plastic sheet glass just a little bit bigger than the window opening so it overlaps slightly onto the wood. Glue this glass directly to the house. Casements will come later.

Window casements are built directly on the house. These casements go on both the inside and the outside to give the illusion of an entire window. These casements can be built with either thin strip wood, textured lace or card.

Windows are the last thing added to a house because they need to go over the wallpaper, paint or other finishing techniques.

Narrow strips of wood or craft matchsticks placed directly on the plastic sheet glass will give the impression of divided glass.

To give the impression of leaded glass, you can paint these wood strips black to resemble iron.

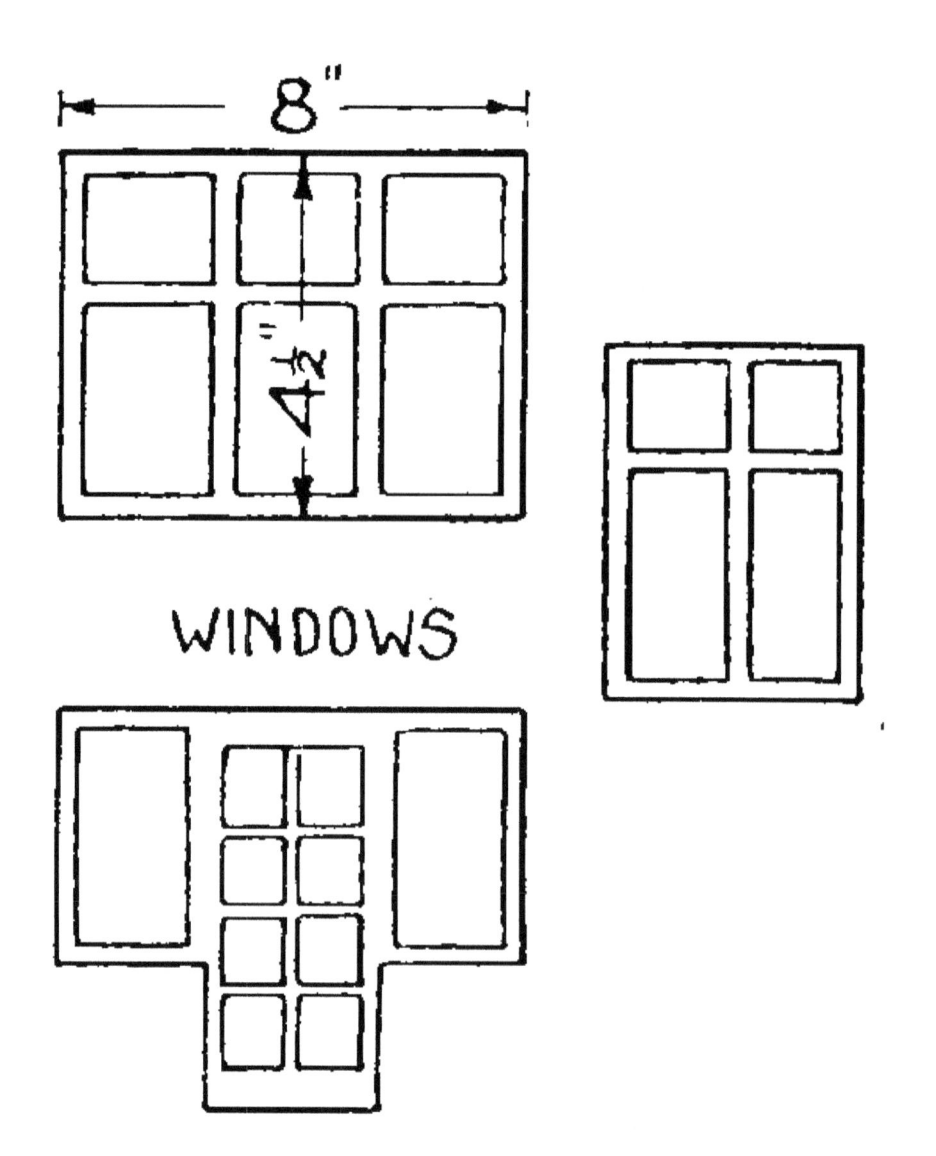

WINDOWS

Bowed Window

The bow window is actually not as hard as it originally seems. For the purposes of strength, it is actually built on semi-circular rings of plywood, surrounded in illustration board with a veneer of cardstock.

The first step in making your bowed window is to prepare straight strips of wood. Strip wood can also be used.

Use figure 9 to mark out and cut six grooves in each piece of wood.

Each groove should be 3/16" wide and 1/8" deep.

Next, you will also need two semicircles to form the top and bottom of the bowed window. The widest point should be 4 ½"

Additionally, cut four semi-circular rings of 4 ¾" and ¼" wide to give the bowed window support as shown in figure 9.

Place the plan so the curve faces the ceiling. Lay out the semicircles for both the top and bottom. Then place the four rings between them.

Attach the strips of wood to the semicircles and rings with small finishing nails and glue.

This provides the framework for your bowed window.

Fig 9

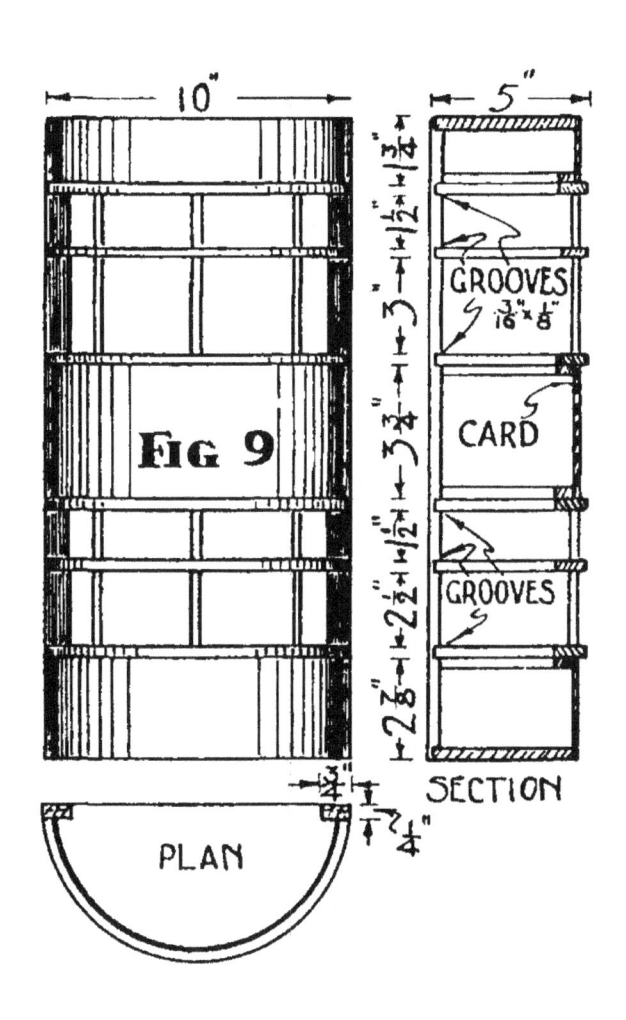

Once dry, score your illustration board lightly. By not cutting all the way through, this board can be curved around the bow window.

Cut out windows where appropriate. Since the illustration board is only there for cosmetic value, you can feel free to cut out as many windows as you want.

The wooden frame provides the actual support.

Windowsill and top rails should be made out of board rather than actual strip wood. Board has the ability to curve around surfaces.

The sills are semi-circular pieces that measure about 5" on the outside diameter and ½" wide.

When finished, glue and screw the bowed window to the front of the dollhouse. For an extra smooth finish, card can be glued to the outside of the bowed window.

CILLS, TOP RAILS ETC

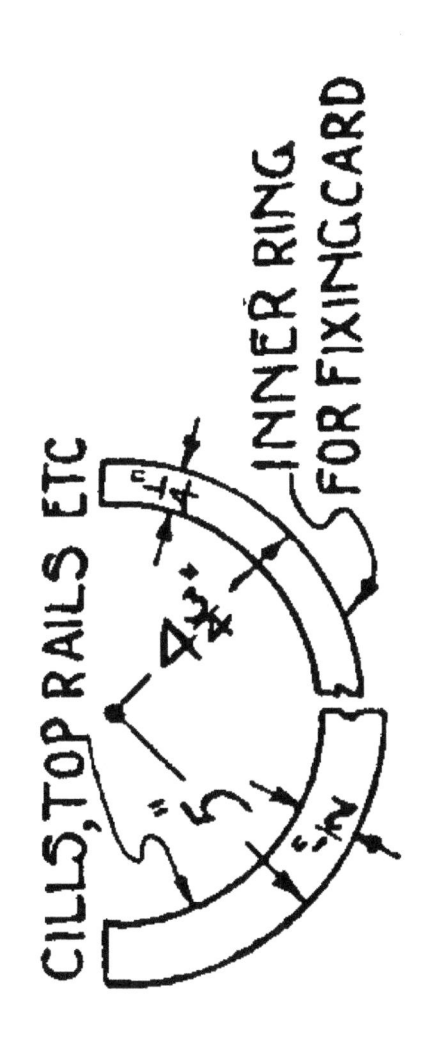

INNER RING FOR FIXING CARD

Stairs

Making all the stairs now enables you to have them available when you are ready for them.

Some technical terminology is needed before the stairs can be made. These words for stairs are the words that will be used throughout the rest of this book.

Stairs have three main parts: stringers, risers, and treads.

'Treads' are the top part of the stairs, or where the foot goes.

'Risers' are the parts of the stairs that lift the treads up from the step below it.

'Stringers' are the sides of the stairs. They support both the treads and risers. Together, these pieces make up the steps. You can see both treads and risers in figure 74.

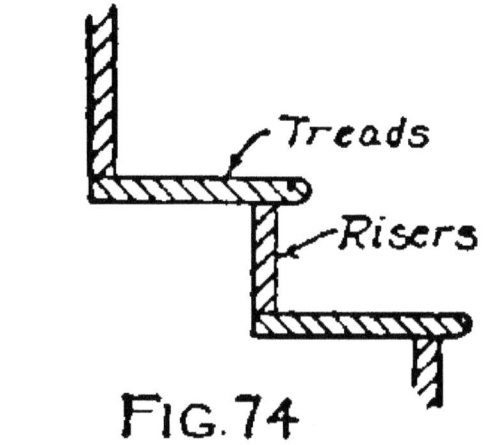

FIG. 74
TREADS AND RISERS.

Although they may look complicated, the stairs used here are some of the easiest to make. A specialized stair shaped stringer is not necessary.

These stairs are known as 'box stairs. Cut two sides for the box stairs, as shown in figure 10.

Each side should measure 1' x 1" X 1 ¼."

Next, cut 12 blocks of ¾" section of wood. Each block should measure 1 ¾."

Then simply glue the blocks to the sides as shown in figure 10.

FIG 10

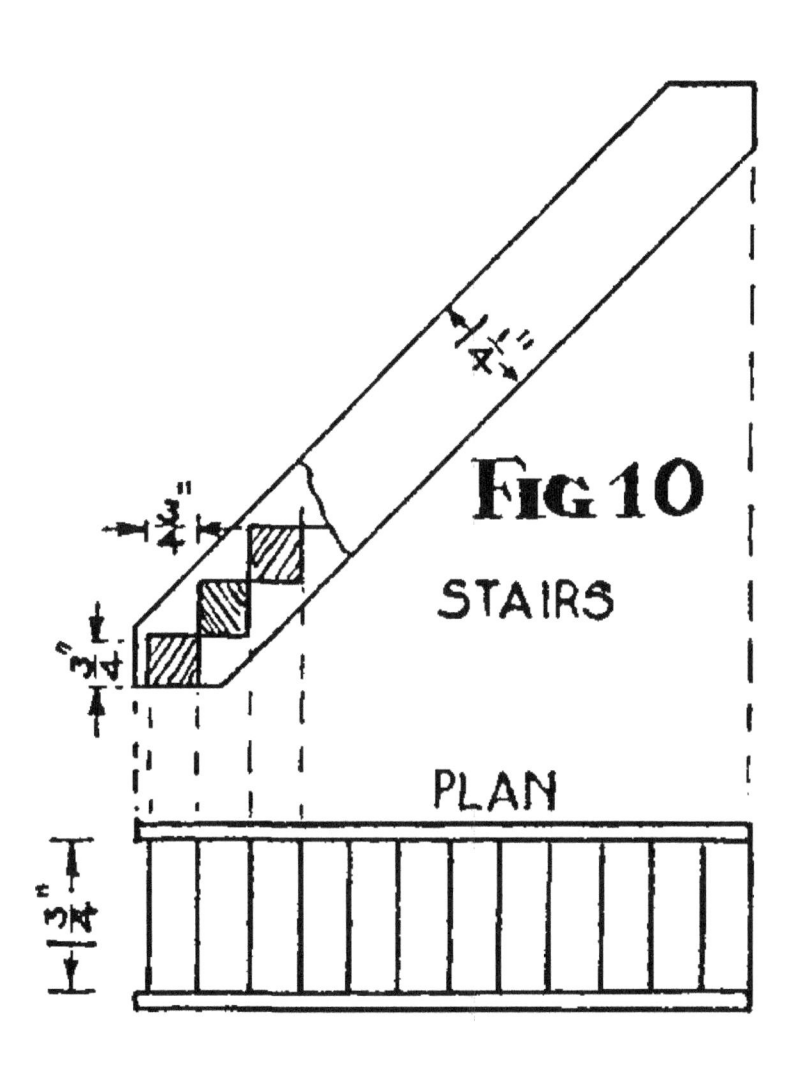

STAIRS

PLAN

Railings

Now that the stair part of the staircase is finished, it's time to add the railings and posts.

The pillar posts are called balustrades.

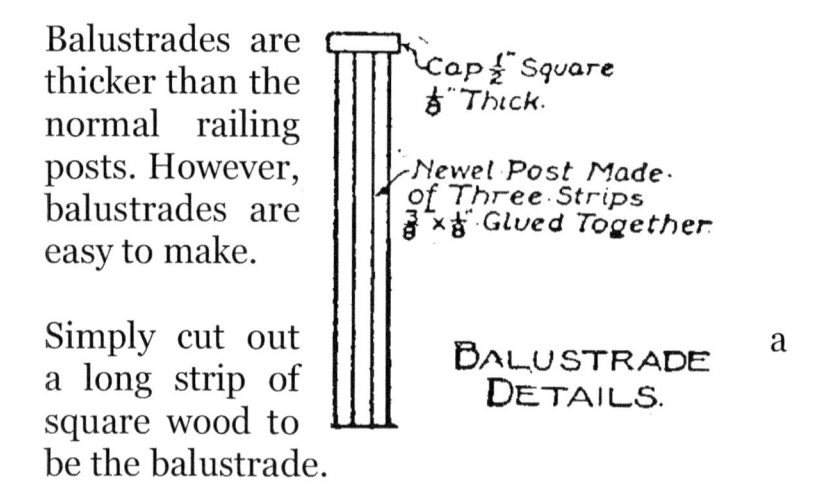

Balustrades are thicker than the normal railing posts. However, balustrades are easy to make.

Simply cut out a long strip of square wood to be the balustrade.

Cap ½" Square ⅛" Thick.

Newel Post Made of Three Strips ⅜" x ⅛" Glued Together

BALUSTRADE DETAILS.

This pillar post can be enhanced with the addition of a slightly larger scrap of wood on top to be the overhang, as well as covering it with toothpicks to create grooves. This gives it a more 'classical column' appearance.

Additionally, you can also use pieces of strip wood or bead 'turnings' to create balustrades.

Because of the delicacy, the turnings that make up the posts between the balustrades are nothing more than simple toothpicks.

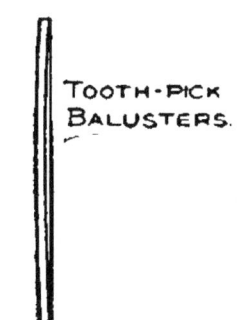

TOOTH-PICK BALUSTERS.

You can use round toothpicks, square craft sticks or even carved toothpicks to get the effect you want.

Simply cut the toothpicks to size and glue them to the stairs.

The railing is made out of a piece of strip wood or skewer.

If possible, you can cut a groove into the top of the railing to keep the toothpicks in line and hide flaws in the height.

If that is not possible, a very thin piece of stripwood or lace trim would work well here. Painted lace will give the illusion of carved wood.

Groove — $\frac{3}{16}$" Wide — $\frac{1}{4}$" Thick

HAND RAIL

Roof

To make the roof, simply cut two pieces of wood square. Each piece of wood has it's own measurements.

The first piece should be 2' 6" x 1' 3 ½" on all sides.

The second piece should be 1' 3 7/8" on all sides.

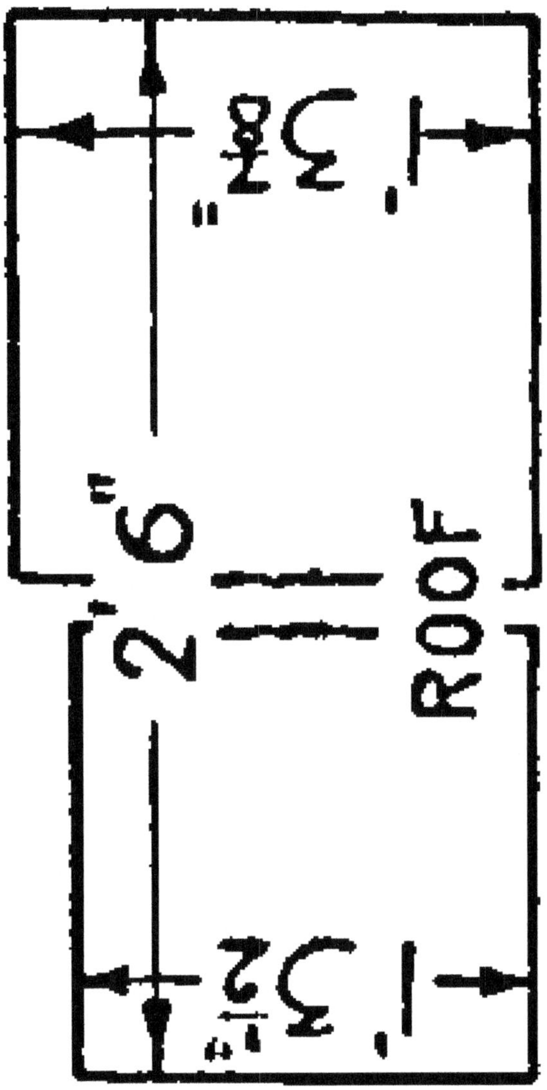
2' 6"
ROOF

Chimney

The easiest way to make a chimney is to build a hollow box. For ease of use, these can be built out of illustration board instead of wood.

The chimney measures 2" x 2" by 2 ½".

This box should have a 'bird mouth' cut into it as seen in figure 92.

This enables the chimney to fit over the ridge on top of the house's roof.

Easy ways to make bricks are covered in the 'Finishing Touches' section of this book.

Fig. 92

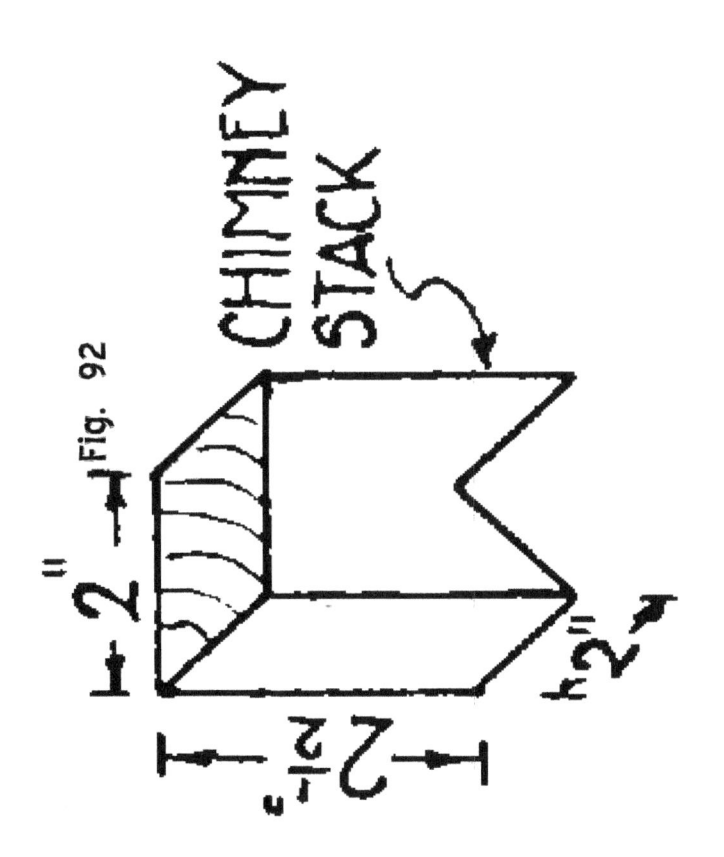

CHIMNEY STACK

2"
2½"
2"

Front Door

Though it's true you can buy a door, you can also make one. The door can be made out of either illustration board or wood.

The dimensions of the door should be 6" x 4," the dimensions of the doorway in partition C. You can finish the door with paint, stripped wood or make it look like any other door you want.

More about doors can be found in the 'Finishing Touches' section of the book.

Assembly

You're finally ready to assemble the house. It goes together in this order:

- Ground Floor
- Outer Walls
- Ground Floor Partitions
- Staircase
- First Floor
- First Floor Partitions
- Bow Window
- Roof
- Back

Congratulations!

You just created a very challenging house with a bowed window.

Finishing Touches

Now we come to one of the most fun parts about having a dollhouse; the decorating. While this is by no means a comprehensive chapter on decorating, decorating alone could fill a book; this will give you a brief overview on how to finish your dollhouse so you can have one you're proud of.

Floors

There are several options for floors in your dollhouse. Which one you choose will depend on your personal taste.

Using Your Home's Natural Wood

If your dollhouse is made of real wood, then you can you can simply use a craft knife and ruler to score the floor so it looks like planks. When you stain the floor, the stain will naturally collect in these grooves giving the illusion of actual planks.

Popsicle Sticks

To make an inexpensive real wood floor, use popsicle sticks with the round ends cut off. Glue them down, and then stain as usual.

Commercial Hardwood Floors

Hardwood floors are available commercially. They are made up thin woods applied to a fabric backing. Since they are genuine, often exotic, woods, they are the most expensive option.

Floor Paper

For a more economical alternative to real wood or tile, consider Floor Paper. Floor Paper simulates the look of tile, wood, parquet and more.

Best of all, you can buy whole books of Floor Paper for the price of the most commercially available hardwood floors.

To see the selection of Floor Paper available from Dollhouse Devotions, go to:

http://www.thisofferisgreat.com/dd

Carpets and Rugs

Carpets can either be bought commercially or simulated with felt.

Throw rugs can be purchased, created with fancy ribbons, scraps of appropriately textured cloth or old fashioned handkerchiefs.

Tile

Tile has to be small enough in scale both thinness and surface. Polymer clay is an excellent choice for tile because it can be created paper thin.

Plastic dollhouse tile sheets or tiled Floor Paper are also good options.

Wall Pictures

No home is complete without pictures.

Pictures can be cut out of magazines and then framed with strip wood to give the illusion of a picture in a frame.

These frames can even be embellished with puffy paint or small rhinestones painted a solid color to represent a fancier frame.

You can also use paper frames to show off your mini artwork.

Brick

There are commercial brick kits you can buy to give the illusions of bricks. These kits feature everything from individual clay bricks to stencils and textured paint.

You can also use sand paper cut into brick shapes and painted the appropriate color. These paper bricks have the advantage of being able to turn around corners.

Brick paper can also be used if you want to cover a large area quickly. Like Floor Paper, brick paper is the most economical alternative. Either you can buy sheets of brick paper or you can purchase a book of Floor Paper that has the appropriate brick pattern in it.

Shingles

In addition to commercially available shingles, there are many other ways to shingle a house.

Again, sand paper can be used by cutting into the appropriate strips and gluing it into place.

Shingle paper can also be used if you're looking to cover large areas quickly.

Doors

Though doors can be purchased commercially, they can also be made with thin stripwood or board.

These handcrafted doors can be created with pieces of board, strip wood, rhinestones or even puffy paint. Simply apply your embellishments and paint to look like wood or painted wood.

A fabric hinge is easily made by gluing a piece of fabric to both the door and the interior of the door way. This hinge can then be covered with trim, wallpaper or paint.

A shiny bead can serve as doorknob.

Stained Glass

This can easily be replicated by printing out the appropriate patterns on computer transparency paper. When you download the patterns for this dollhouse, you will receive some stained glass patterns in a few days. Size to fit, then print out.

Wallpaper

Wallpaper is one of the most popular ways to finish the inside of a dollhouse. While sheets of wallpaper are available individually, wallpaper books can be purchased at a fraction of the price.

Be sure to check out Dollhouse Devotions' assortment of wallpaper books here:

http://www.thisofferisgreat.com/dd

A Note from Dollhouse Devotions:

If you enjoyed this book, please consider leaving a review.

If you have any suggestions on how to make future books better, you can contact us at:

info@newartspublishing.com

You can also download your free patterns from this book at

http://www.thisofferisgreat.com/dhmodern

Don't forget to see all our dollhouse books including plans and wallpapers and floor papers.

http://www.thisofferisgreat.com/dd

Printed in Great Britain
by Amazon